Utah

By Trudi Strain Trueit

Subject Consultant
Bonne Rogers
Education Specialist
Utah State Historical Society
Salt Lake City, Utah

Reading Consultant
Cecilia Minden-Cupp, PhD
Former Director of the Language and Literacy Program
Harvard Graduate School of Education
Cambridge, Massachusetts

Children's Press®
A Division of Scholastic Inc.
New York   Toronto   London   Auckland   Sydney
Mexico City   New Delhi   Hong Kong
Danbury, Connecticut

Designer: Herman Adler
Photo Researcher: Caroline Anderson
The photo on the cover shows rock formations in Utah's Bryce Canyon
National Park

Library of Congress Cataloging-in-Publication Data

Trueit, Trudi Strain.
  Utah / Trudi Strain Trueit.
    p. cm. — (Rookie read-about geography)
  Includes index.
  ISBN 13: 978-0-531-12574-8 (lib. bdg.)   978-0-531-16818-9 (pbk.)
  ISBN 10: 0-531-12574-2 (lib. bdg.)   0-531-16818-2 (pbk.)
  1. Utah—Juvenile literature. 2. Utah—Geography—Juvenile
literature. I. Title. II. Series.
  F826.3.T78 2007
  979.2—dc22   2006017610

CHILDREN'S PRESS, and ROOKIE READ-ABOUT®, and associated
logos are trademarks and/or registered trademarks of Scholastic Library
Publishing. SCHOLASTIC and associated logos are trademarks and/or
registered trademarks of Scholastic Inc.
1 2 3 4 5 6 7 8 9 10 R 16 15 14 13 12 11 10 09 08 07

Where can you find canyons every color of the rainbow? Which state has rocks shaped like castles and alien spaceships? It's Utah!

The state of Utah is in the western United States. It is bordered by Arizona, Colorado, Idaho, Nevada, New Mexico, and Wyoming.

Can you find Utah on the map?

CANADA

WASHINGTON
OREGON
IDAHO
MONTANA
NORTH DAKOTA
MINNESOTA
NEW HAMPSHIRE
VERMONT
MAINE
MICHIGAN
WISCONSIN
WYOMING
SOUTH DAKOTA
NEW YORK
MASSACHUSETTS
RHODE ISLAND
CONNECTICUT
NEW JERSEY
NEVADA
UTAH
NEBRASKA
IOWA
PENNSYLVANIA
OHIO
INDIANA
WEST VIRGINIA
DELAWARE
MARYLAND
Washington, D.C.
CALIFORNIA
COLORADO
KANSAS
MISSOURI
ILLINOIS
KENTUCKY
VIRGINIA
NORTH CAROLINA
ARIZONA
NEW MEXICO
OKLAHOMA
ARKANSAS
TENNESSEE
SOUTH CAROLINA
TEXAS
MISSISSIPPI
ALABAMA
GEORGIA
LOUISIANA
FLORIDA

North
West   East
South

ALASKA   CANADA
MEXICO

HAWAII

5

Four Corners Monument

Four Corners Monument is the only place in the United States where four states meet at one point.

If you visit, you can touch Utah, Arizona, Colorado, and New Mexico at the same time!

Native Americans were the first people to live in Utah.

Europeans came in the mid-1700s. The earliest settlers were a religious group called the Mormons.

A Mormon family in Utah in 1869

Sego lilies

Utah's state flower is the sego lily.

The state bird is the California gull.

The Rocky Mountains
cross central and
northeastern Utah.
Bears, cougars, eagles,
deer, and foxes live in
these mountains.

Pine trees grow here,
including the blue spruce.
The blue spruce is Utah's
state tree.

Utah's Rocky Mountains

13

A Gila monster

Southwestern Utah is a dry, rocky area. Cactuses grow here.

Rattlesnakes, prairie dogs, desert tortoises, and Gila monsters live in southwestern Utah. The Gila monster is the only poisonous lizard in the United States.

The Colorado and Green
rivers flow through
Utah. Rivers have carved
many colorful canyons
throughout the state.

The Colorado River

Hoodoos in Utah

Rivers, wind, and rain have worn down rocks in Utah to make strange shapes. If you visit, you can see tall, stone towers called hoodoos.

Utah's Great Salt Lake
is the biggest saltwater
lake in North America.
It's much saltier than
the ocean.

No fish live in the lake,
but it is home to tiny
animals called brine shrimp.

The Great Salt Lake

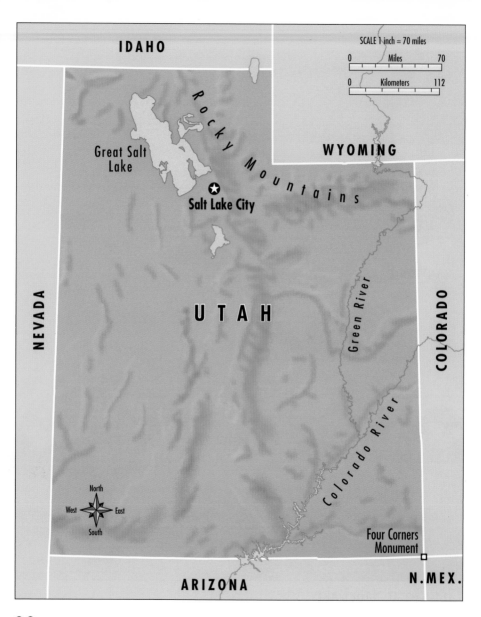

IDAHO

SCALE 1 inch = 70 miles

| 0 | Miles | 70 |

| 0 | Kilometers | 112 |

Rocky Mountains

Great Salt Lake

WYOMING

⭐ Salt Lake City

NEVADA

UTAH

Green River

COLORADO

Colorado River

North

West ✴ East

South

Four Corners Monument □

ARIZONA

N.MEX.

Salt Lake City is the largest city in Utah. It's also the state capital.

In 2002, Salt Lake City hosted the Winter Olympic Games.

Many people in Utah
work in hotels, restaurants,
hospitals, and schools.
Some people work for
the U.S. government.

Utah factories make
parts for computers,
cars, and airplanes.

A worker in a Utah computer factory

A boy picks apples on a Utah farm.

Some Utah farmers
grow apples, cherries,
and peaches.

Others raise beans,
potatoes, and tomatoes.

Utah is filled with amazing places to explore!

What will you do first when you get there?

Visitors hiking past hoodoos in Utah

Words You Know

Colorado River

Four Corners Monument

Gila monster

Great Salt Lake

hoodoos

Mormons

Rocky Mountains

sego lilies

Index

About the Author

Trudi Strain Trueit is a former television news reporter and weather forecaster. She has written more than forty fiction and nonfiction books for children. Ms. Trueit lives near Seattle, Washington.

Photo Credits

Photographs © 2007: Alamy Images: 29 (Russ Bishop), 6, 30 top right (Ron Niebrugge); AP/Wide World Photos/Douglas C. Pizac: 25; Art Resource, NY/ The New York Public Library: 9, 31 top right; Corbis Images: 26 (Dewitt Jones), 14, 30 bottom left (David A. Northcott), 21, 30 bottom right (Scott T. Smith); David R. Frazier: cover; Dembinsky Photo Assoc./Rod Planck: 3; Minden Pictures/Tim Fitzharris: 10, 31 bottom right; Ric Ergenbright: 18, 31 top left; Superstock, Inc.: 13, 31 bottom left (age fotostock), 17, 30 top left (Tom Benoit).

Maps by Bob Italiano